GW00660709

Perfect
TUSCANY

FABIO MUZZI

HALSGROVE

First published in Great Britain in 2008

Copyright © Fabio Muzzi 2008

All rights reserved. No part of this publication may be reproduced,
stored in a retrieval system, or transmitted in any form or by any
means without the prior permission of the copyright holder.

British Library Cataloguing-in-Publication Data
A CIP record for this title is available from the British Library

ISBN 978 1 84114 746 8

HALSGROVE
Halsgrove House
Ryelands Industrial Estate
Bagley Road, Wellington, Somerset TA21 9PZ
United Kingdom
Tel: 01823 653777   Fax: 01823 216796
email: sales@halsgrove.com
website: www.halsgrove.com

Printed and bound by
D'Auria Industrie Grafiche, Italy

FOREWORD

This book is dedicated to those dreaming of being part of this magical and authentic land, to those dreaming of being seduced by its beauty and simplicity and of moving with the rhythm of its colours, fragrances and history.

Tuscany remains a protected haven where nature silently has reigned for centuries, a time immortalized on canvas by painters in the fifteenth and sixteenth centuries, a true harmony of colours, forms and landscape. A perfect and consistent composition where people live surrounded by a breezy tranquillity, witnesses of a rich, artistic and cultural past, rejoicing in this still unchanged world.

In Tuscany time seems to stand still. Every view seems to present an enticing spectacle. Sometimes the landscape awakes dressed in a mantle of mist, like a sea of clouds fading into an infinite red glowing heaven. A dog is barking far away and only the smoke of chimneys curling upwards reminds us of civilization.

Tuscany represents so many different things to the thousands of people from all over the world who visit each year, searching for the genuine, for simple pleasures, real emotions and the sweet things of life.

Tuscany is a mixture of smells and sights to delight the senses and increase the serenity of the spirit.

Tuscany is a line of cypress trees standing gracefully along winding roads and dusty paths, leading our steps towards stone houses which still dominate this unspoilt land.

Tuscany, both open and reserved, keeps the mystery of its life and rich past hidden in the very heart of its forests and castles.

Tuscany is the place for healthy pleasures, home of the Chianti wine from vineyards stretching as far as you can see, illuminated with an intense and warm autumnal light as if nature itself is on fire.

Tuscany is atmosphere. A living and breathing atmosphere. You can be moved, surprised and wholly immersed in its landscapes and medieval villages. You can meet the warm-hearted villagers and have with them a bottle of local wine and a slice of pecorino cheese – people proud to be Tuscan.

Tuscany is a hymn to peace and love. To love because people from Tuscany after the medieval fighting period preserved so fully their identity and their culinary, artistic and cultural tradition. To peace, because the love of nature and the search for a good way of life is important to all inhabitants.

Tuscany is a philosophy of life, shared by countless others who are devoted to this precious corner of Italy where you willingly leave a little piece of your heart and spirit.

Tuscany is an invitation to dreams and travels. Let yourself be seduced…

Valérie Dorlhiac

INTRODUCTION

Tuscany is the cradle of European civilization. Here the Renaissance was born, and its medieval cities – including Florence, Pisa and Siena – remain packed with unrivalled art and architecture. And yet, perhaps the greatest glory of Tuscany lies in its landscapes. It is a big region of nearly 23,000 sq km, and is not really just one landscape but several. Chianti, famed for its vineyards, lies in the middle and is probably the best-known part to visitors. But Tuscany stretches from the mountains of the north to the bare clay hills of the Crete Senesi south of Siena, and is bounded on the west by a long and varied sea coast. These landscapes are not only very different from each other, but can appear quite changed within themselves, between the seasons and even at different times of day.

Large tracts of Tuscany have never been wealthy and its farmers have been too poor to use intensive agricultural methods. The happy consequence is that the countryside can appear to be frozen in time, olive groves mixing with vineyards and fields of cereals to feed the livestock. Tall cypress trees march through the landscape and have become probably the most recognized symbol of the region, but it is blessed with an abundance of other flora and fauna which have flourished alongside traditional farming.

The 'best of the old' survives strongly in the Tuscan culture. Nowhere is this seen more colourfully than in the many Tuscan festivals which celebrate historical events, sometimes many centuries past. Possibly the most famous is the Palio in Siena, which may have its origins in Roman times, although it was first recorded in 1283. It is a horserace run around the Campo – central square – in the city on 2 July and 16 August: the winner is awarded a banner, or Palio, in front of several thousand eager spectators.

Nevertheless, Tuscany is part of the modern world: its cities and towns thrive, its manufacturing economy is strong, its tourism industry enormous. It does not prettify its heritage, but treats it as part of a living tradition. It is this above all that makes Tuscany such an alluring and rewarding place to photograph: a thousand years of beauty are revealed before you as you stand in the Tuscan sun of the twenty-first century.

The Crete Senesi in springtime.

DEDICATION

This book is dedicated to the stunning beauty of my homeland Tuscany. I have worked for more than twenty years and travelled many thousands of miles to rolling farmland where time has seemingly stood still, returning again and again to capture its subtle changes of light, colour and climate.

This book is also dedicated to the memory of my mother Marisa, to my wife Valérie and to my daughters Bianca and Lea.

The medieval Castiglione della Pescaia shortly before sunset. The village lies on the coast, on the edge of the Maremma, reclaimed marshland in Southern Tuscany.

The Val d'Orcia, near San Quirico d'Orcia, in high summer.

An almost stereotypical view of the Tuscan countryside, with straw bales and a
cypress-surrounded farmhouse under a brilliant blue sky.

Snow in Tuscany is a rare event.

Cypresses along a twisting road, near Monticchiello in the Val d'Orcia.

Winter in Tuscany often means mist and fog – here filling the valleys, allowing the hilltops to peep through as in a fairytale. The view is near Monte Oliveto Maggiore, a medieval abbey on the road between Asciano and Buonconvento.

Spring, with the traditional yellow colsa flower. Some say that the best time of year to see the Tuscan countryside is when the wildflowers bloom in May and June.

Leonina in the Crete Senesi, south of Siena, in autumn.

Twin cypresses invite the eye into a characteristic Tuscan spring scene.

The Val d'Orcia in autumn.

Cypresses in the Chianti Classico region, beneath a stunning autumn sky.

Dawn breaks over Belvedere farm, near San Quirico d'Orcia.

The campanile of Pisa Cathedral – the famous Leaning Tower – illuminated with thousands of candles during the celebrations of the city's patron Saint Ranieri.

A winter sunrise in the Chianti Classico, famous for its vineyards and wine.

Little hills dusted with snow as if with a brush in the Val d'Orcia.

Siena. Medieval alleyways fan out from the Piazza del Campo.

A sunset view of Siena, dominated by the Torre del Mangia – the belltower of the
Palazzo Pubblico – and the campanile and dome of the cathedral (Duomo).

A field goes under the plough in the autumn.

A hilltop farm shivers in a snowy sunrise near Asciano in the Crete Senesi.

Cypresses are often planted as windbreaks along roadsides, as here near Monticchiello.

Said to be one of the most moving sights in Tuscany, the remote church of Chiesina di Vitaleta with a little farm beside it.

(*Left*) Golden cornfields surround a stand of cypresses.

Near San Quirico
d'Orcia – a wintry dawn.

The contrasting seasons bring changing mantles of colour on this landscape in the Crete Senesi. Spring. *[left]* Summer. *[top]* Autumn. *[bottom]*

One of the best times to appreciate the delicate beauty of Tuscany at its finest is at first light on a spring morning.
Ville di Corsano, near Siena.

A misty spring sunrise brings stunning light and colours.

Poppies are a traditional harbinger of springtime in Tuscany.

Billowing hills of growing corn.

Beneath snow on the high hills, a farmstead in the Val d'Orcia catches the last rays of the setting sun.

Moonrise near Mucigliani, in the Crete Senesi.

A Crete Senesi doorway, festooned with roses.

(Right) Poppy-strewn fields introduce richer hues to the otherwise green landscape.

Ribbons of windblown snow near Mucigliani.

The sun breaks through the mist in the Crete Senesi.

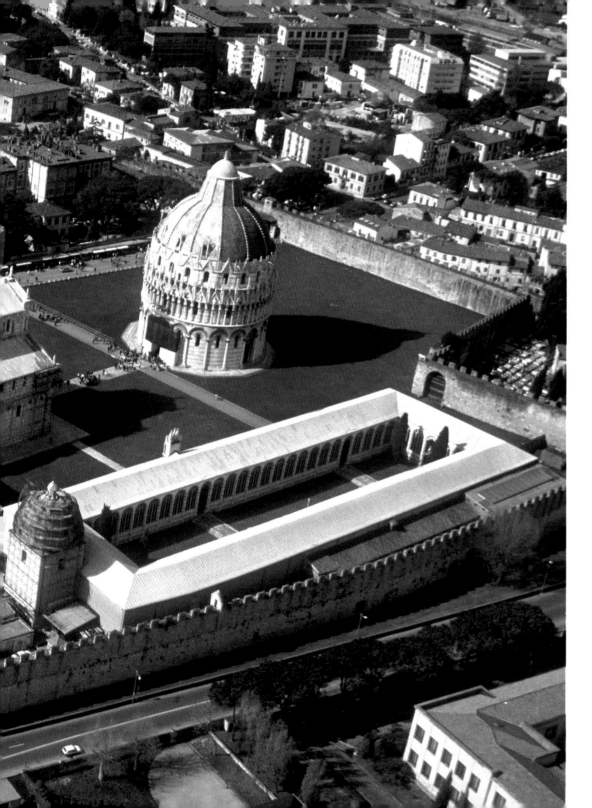

An aerial view of the core of historic Pisa and the main square, Piazza dei Miracoli, with the campanile, cathedral and domed baptistry.

September and grapes are gathered at Lilliano farm, Chianti Classico.

An old ox cart is pressed into service to transport grapes at Montechiaro farm, Chianti Classico.

November and time to harvest olives for oil at Vignano farm, Chianti Classico.

The dying embers of a glowing autumn day near Mucigliani.

The snaking, ancient roadway near Monticchiello, Val d'Orcia.

Tuscan dreamscapes – hilltop settlements floating on the early-morning mists.

A landscape of vibrant colour in the Chianti valley.

A closer view of the fields and vineyards around Grignano farm near Panzano, on an early autumn morning.

The neat rows of red and golden vines at Cecchi farm near the village of Castellina in the Chianti valley.

As October draws on so the early morning mists become more prevalent: the vineyards
near the village of Radda in the Chianti valley.

The serried rows of vines sweep the eye forward near the Chianti-valley village of Topina.

'Chianti' is not one wine but several. Today there are over 7000 registered vineyards in the Chianti region. These are near Topina.

Near Poggibonsi on an early autumn morning.

(Right) The medieval hamlet of Castel di Tonda
near Castelfalfi in the Era valley.

Near Pienza, in the Val d'Orcia, birthplace of Pope Pius II in 1405, who had it redesigned as a model Renaissance town.

(Right) To many this view will be extremely familiar: this part of the Val d'Orcia was used as a location for the film 'Gladiator'.

From a terrace in Pienza, it is possible to admire this idyllic scene of the Tuscan countryside on a spring morning.

The traditional yellow Colsa flower blooms profusely in spring.

Colsa and poppies form a colourful foreground to this switchback Tuscan road.

The Val d'Orcia on a late spring afternoon, the shadows lengthening evocatively across the landscape.

A hilltop farm at the end of a cypress avenue basks under a brilliant blue spring sky.

A solitary cypress stands before undulating swathes of colsa.

The sulla flower adds a dash of vivid purple to this springtime scene near Pienza.

This landscape in the Val d'Orcia appears to have been unchanged for centuries: it is easy to imagine ancient Romans marching along this road.

(Right) A farmstead near Bettolle in the Valdichiana valley.

The Chiesina di Vitaleta in the Val d'Orcia, with a foreground of spring poppies.

A succession of lonely hilltop farmsteads roll out in a seemingly endless view.

A characteristic Val d'Orcia landscape with a remote farm perched on a hillock surrounded by cypresses.

Angry thunderclouds gather over the Val d'Orcia in spring.

The Chiesina di Vitaleta is thrown into high relief by the dark clouds of an approaching storm.

The purple sulla flower mixing with springtime wheat.

The Orciano Pisano valley in the spring.

High summer in central Tuscany.

Belvedere farm in the middle distance, with Pienza looming on the hilltop beyond.

Golden light, late in the afternoon of a hot summer's day: a thunderstorm will come soon.

(*Left*) Late afternoon at a farm in the Val d'Orcia near Pienza.

(*Right*) Belvedere farm at a foggy winter sunrise: a summation of all that is quiet and relaxing about Tuscany.

Vibrant sunflowers dancing in the summer breeze.

Red poppies, wheat fields and a line of cypress trees: all in perfect 'Tuscan style'.

A vineyard-filled landscape near Panzano on an early autumn morning.

Ripe corn under a baking Tuscan sun.

The solitaire. This single cypress towers over a panorama of the Arbia valley in springtime.

(Right) Castel di Spaltenna near Gaiole emerges from October mist.

August, and a romantic scene of great white clouds floating in an azure sky above undulating wheat fields.

(Left) The Crete Senesi in summer, near Mucigliani.

(Right) One of the most stunning religious sites in Tuscany: Monte Oliveto Maggiore, in the heart of the Crete Senesi. Founded by the Olivetan order in 1313, the abbey church was built in the fifteenth century.

Spring near Volterra in the Valdera valley.

An aerial view of the beautiful abbey of Sant' Antimo. The alabaster interior changes with the light conditions and is best seen in the early morning or late afternoon.

A panoramic view at the mouth of the Arno in the Tyrrhenian Sea: an old fisher-house, Marina di Pisa, dawn.

Spring, early morning, charming light, soft not invasive fog, gentle repetitive hills with characteristic farms.

A specialist cellar in Chianti Classico for the production of the sweet Vin Santo.

The Castello di Brolio, north east of Siena, has been owned since the twelfth century by the Ricasoli family.

A picturesque view of a farm in the Val d'Orcia.

A wintry view before a storm on the coast near Livorno.

(Right) A more placid spring sea. The Calafuria coast of the Tyrrhenian Sea.

The vineyards on an early autumn morning near Radda in the Chianti valley.

Late afternoon in the Arbia valley.

Autumnal tones near
Monti di Sopra, Chianti
valley.

A farm seemingly surfs on an evocative sea of fog.

(Right) Monteriggioni. The walls of the town were built between 1213 and 1219, as a key part of the defence of Siena against Florence.

A gentle October haze descends on Chianti Classico.

Vineyards and trees gain the tints of red and yellow in the idyllic Tuscan autumn.

Autumn near Monticchiello, a tiny medieval village with a thirteenth-century church.

A stream of white clouds above wheat fields and cypresses.

Poggio al Frati farm, near the Arbia valley, in spring.

The Crete Senesi on an early spring morning near Mucigliani.

A bird's-eye view of Badia a Coltbuono, originally a medieval abbey and now the centre of a wine-producing estate.

(Right) The city of Florence, one of the world's architectural jewels. The River Arno and the Ponte Vecchio are in the foreground.

Although only a small town, the soaring towers of San Gimignano have brought it international fame.

Known as the 'City of Beautiful Towers', fourteen of San Gimignano's medieval towers survive.

An early morning
autumnal view of Sant'
Antimo nestling in the
Val d'Orcia.

Leonina in the Crete Senesi: autumn.

A wider view in springtime of Leonina, the mist hovering in the valley below.

A soft, thin mantle of snow lies on the olive groves and cypress trees of Biondi Santi farm near Montalcino in the Arbia valley.

Foggy winter sunrise at La Pievina in the Crete Senesi.

A farm emerges as an island in a sea of ethereal winter fog.

(*Right*) This farmstead on its ridge stands aloof above the swirling mists.

An all-too-transient dawn, just captured before the colours of the 'painted' clouds faded to monochrome.

The scarlet flash of spring poppies.

An aerial view of Siena, with perhaps 35,000 spectators watching the famous Palio in the main square, 'Il Campo'

Pienza. The medieval town was originally called Corsignano but when Pope Pius II had it rebuilt in the mid 1400s, he renamed it after himself.

The Belvedere farm, in the Val d'Orcia, at sunrise.

A smooth field of young corn contrasts with the rounded hillocks and cypress trees beyond.

Spring is bursting into life in this early morning scene.

The vineyards of Chianti Classico in autumn.

Sunflowers announce proudly the arrival of summer in Tuscany.

The ruined abbey of San Galgano, in the centre of the Merse valley. Galgano was a worldly knight who became a hermit and was declared a saint in 1185, fewer than thirty-five years before the abbey was begun.

Poppies at Belvedere farm.

A gentle autumn.

A dramatic sunrise near Mucigliani, in the Crete Senesi.

Silver tones of winter come to the Tuscan countryside.

(*Right*) An early morning in winter, Mucigliani.

Near La Foce in the Val d'Orcia. La Foce was the home of the celebrated writer Iris Origo, author of *Merchant of Prato*.

Sunset over Pienza.

A traditional Tuscan farm, complete with a flock of sheep, in the Crete Senesi.

A field of poppies amidst lush green.

Bronze foliage of autumn vineyards in Chianti Classico.

A carpet of spring flowers surrounds the abbey church of Sant' Antimo.

The yellow ginestra blossoms in the foreground of Chiesina di Vitaleta.

Delicate poppies and defiant cypresses.

Quintessential sunflowers and a phalanx of cypress trees. Perfect Tuscany.